Diplodocus

by Daniel Cohen

Consultant:
Brent Breithaupt
Director
Geological Museum
University of Wyoming

Bridgestone Books
an imprint of Capstone Press
Mankato, Minnesota

Bridgestone Books are published by Capstone Press
151 Good Counsel Drive, P.O. Box 669, Mankato, Minnesota 56002
http://www.capstone-press.com

Library of Congress Cataloging-in-Publication Data
Cohen, Daniel, 1936–
    Diplodocus / by Daniel Cohen.
    p. cm.—(Discovering dinosaurs)
    Summary: Describes what is known of the physical characteristics, behavior, and habitat of
this long-necked and long-tailed dinosaur.
    Includes bibliographical references and index.
    ISBN 0-7368-1621-6 (hardcover)
    1. Diplodocus—Juvenile literature. [1. Diplodocus. 2. Dinosaurs.] I. Title.
QE862.S3 .C562 2003
567.913—dc21   2002010557

Editorial Credits
Erika Shores, editor; Karen Risch, product planning editor; Linda Clavel, series designer;
    Patrick D. Dentinger, cover production designer; Angi Gahler, production artist;
    Alta Schaffer, photo researcher

Photo Credits
All Rights Reserved, Photo Archives, Denver Museum of Nature and Science, 4–5, 8–9, 14
Hulton/Archive Photos by Getty Images, 18
Index Stock Imagery/RO-MA Stock, 6
The Natural History Museum, 10, 12, 20
Patrick D. Dentinger, cover, 1

1 2 3 4 5 6 08 07 06 05 04 03

Table of Contents

Diplodocus. 5

The World of Diplodocus 7

Parts of Diplodocus. 9

What Diplodocus Ate 11

Traveling in Herds 13

End of Diplodocus 15

Discovering Diplodocus 17

Andrew Carnegie 19

A Famous Dinosaur 21

Hands On: Diplodocus Tail 22

Words to Know 23

Read More 24

Internet Sites 24

Index. 24

Diplodocus compared to a
5-foot-tall (1.5-meter-tall) human

Diplodocus

Diplodocus (dip-LOH-doh-kus) belonged to a group of giant dinosaurs called sauropods (SORE-oh-pods). Diplodocus is one of the longest sauropods ever discovered. Diplodocus was about 90 feet (27 meters) long from head to tail.

The World of Diplodocus

Diplodocus lived about 150 million years ago. Earth looked different during the time of Diplodocus. Earth's landmasses were closer together. The climate was warm and wet. Giant ferns, gingkos, and other tropical plants covered the land.

tropical
related to warm and wet weather

tail

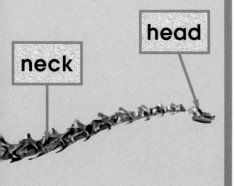

neck

head

Parts of Diplodocus

Diplodocus had a small head and mouth. Its neck was very long. Its thick body stood on four strong legs. Diplodocus had a long, whiplike tail. The tail probably helped Diplodocus balance its long neck. Diplodocus also may have used its tail to protect itself.

What Diplodocus Ate

Diplodocus was a herbivore. It ate plants. It spent much of its time eating. Its mouth was too small to eat a lot of food at once. Diplodocus ate leaves. It then swallowed stones. The stones in the dinosaur's stomach helped grind up the leaves. The leaves could then be digested.

digest
to break down food by the body

Traveling in Herds

Diplodocus probably traveled in herds. A young Diplodocus had to stay close to the herd. Meat-eating dinosaurs may have tried to kill a young Diplodocus. An adult Diplodocus was too big for a meat-eating dinosaur to attack.

herd
a group of animals

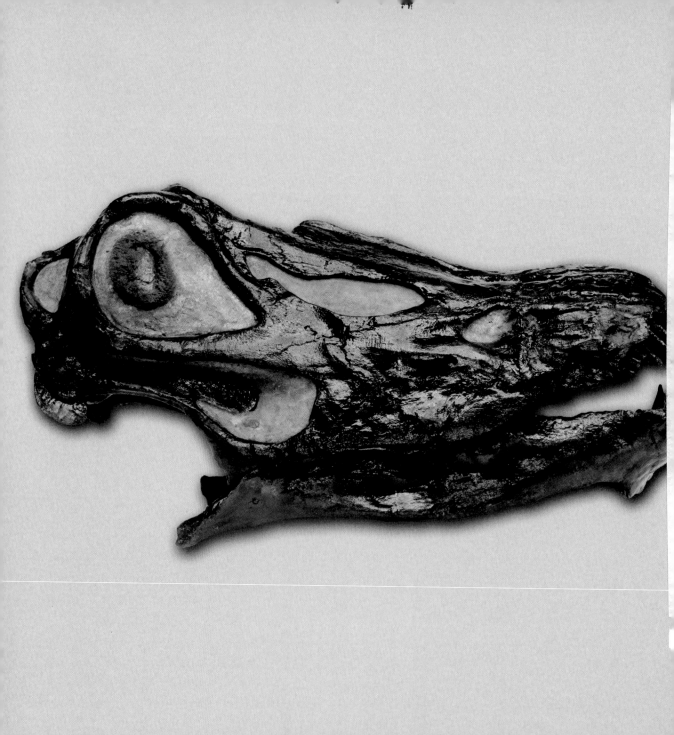

End of Diplodocus

Diplodocus and some other giant sauropods became extinct about 135 million years ago. Scientists are not sure why these dinosaurs died out.

extinct
no longer living anywhere in the world

Montana

Wyoming

Utah Colorado

UNITED STATES

☐ Areas where Diplodocus
fossils have been found

Discovering Diplodocus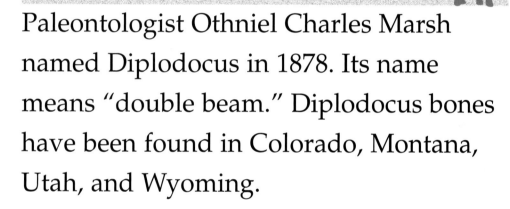

Paleontologist Othniel Charles Marsh named Diplodocus in 1878. Its name means "double beam." Diplodocus bones have been found in Colorado, Montana, Utah, and Wyoming.

Andrew Carnegie

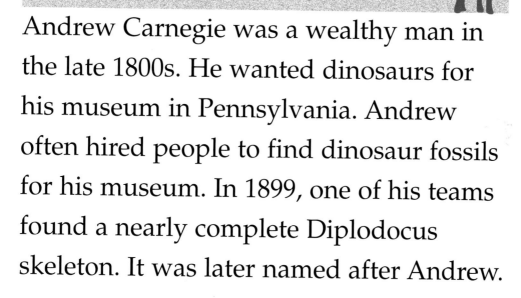

Andrew Carnegie was a wealthy man in the late 1800s. He wanted dinosaurs for his museum in Pennsylvania. Andrew often hired people to find dinosaur fossils for his museum. In 1899, one of his teams found a nearly complete Diplodocus skeleton. It was later named after Andrew.

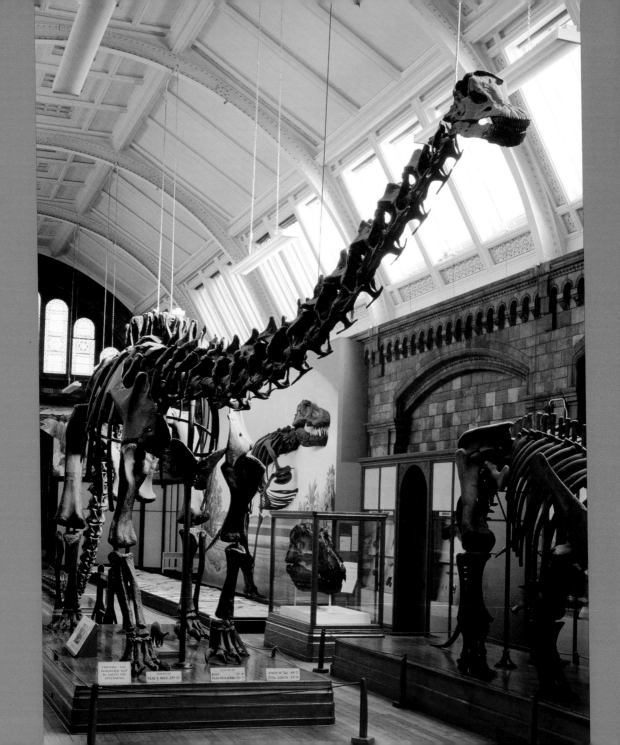

A Famous Dinosaur

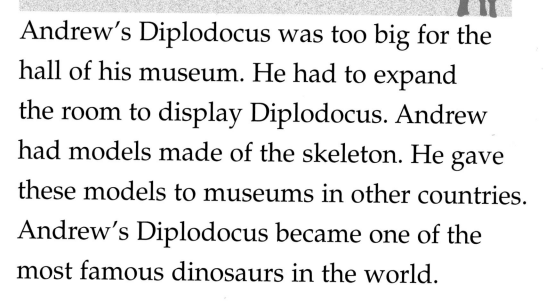

Andrew's Diplodocus was too big for the hall of his museum. He had to expand the room to display Diplodocus. Andrew had models made of the skeleton. He gave these models to museums in other countries. Andrew's Diplodocus became one of the most famous dinosaurs in the world.

Hands On: Diplodocus Tail

Diplodocus had a very long tail. It may have held its tail off the ground. Some scientists think the tail balanced the neck of this long, heavy dinosaur. Try this activity to see how the neck and tail of Diplodocus worked together.

What You Need

An adult to help
Toothpicks
Cardboard tube
Straw
Scissors
Tape
Small marshmallow

What You Do

1. Ask an adult to poke four toothpicks into the cardboard tube. The toothpicks should be arranged like the legs of Diplodocus.
2. Cut the straw in half. Tape half of the straw to the inside of the tube. Part of the straw should stick out from the tube. This is the neck of Diplodocus.
3. Poke a small marshmallow onto the end of the straw. This is the head of Diplodocus. Does your dinosaur stand up with the head attached?
4. Your dinosaur needs a tail to balance its heavy head and neck. Tape the other piece of straw to the other end of the tube to make a tail. Now does your dinosaur stand up?

Words to Know

climate (KLYE-mit)—the usual weather in a place

dinosaur (DYE-na-sore)—an extinct land reptile; dinosaurs lived on Earth for more than 150 million years.

fossil (FOSS-uhl)—the remains or traces of something that once lived; bones and footprints can be fossils.

herbivore (HUR-buh-vor)—an animal that eats plants

scientist (SYE-uhn-tist)—a person who studies the world around us

Read More

Goecke, Michael P. *Diplodocus.* A Buddy Book. Edina, Minn.: Abdo, 2002.

Matthews, Rupert. *Diplodocus.* Gone Forever. Chicago: Heinemann Library, 2003.

Olshevsky, George, and Sandy Fritz. *Diplodocus.* Discovering Dinosaurs. North Mankato, Minn.: Smart Apple Media, 2002.

Internet Sites

Track down many sites about Diplodocus.
Visit the FACT HOUND at *http://www.facthound.com*

IT IS EASY! IT IS FUN!

1) Go to *http://www.facthound.com*
2) Type in: 0736816216
3) Click on "FETCH IT" and FACT HOUND will find several links hand-picked by our editors.

Relax and let our pal FACT HOUND do the research for you!

Index

Carnegie, Andrew, 19, 21
climate, 7
Earth, 7
extinct, 15
head, 5, 9
herbivore, 11
herd, 13

landmasses, 7
Marsh, Othniel Charles, 17
models, 21
neck, 9
plants, 7, 11
sauropod, 5, 15
stones, 11

ל"ס